Hard Letters and Folded Wings

poems by

Martha Catherine Brenckle

Finishing Line Press
Georgetown, Kentucky

Hard Letters and Folded Wings

for my daughters, Jessica and Nikki
for my grandchildren, Avi and Max
and especially and always for my wife, Patty

Copyright © 2019 by Martha Catherine Brenckle
ISBN 978-1-64662-050-0 First Edition
All rights reserved under International and Pan-American Copyright Conventions. No part of this book may be reproduced in any manner whatsoever without written permission from the publisher, except in the case of brief quotations embodied in critical articles and reviews.

ACKNOWLEDGMENTS

"Constructing Border Quilts" in *Bryant Literary Review*
"Phantom Limbs" and "The House Comes Apart" in *Burningword Literary Magazine*
"Aiding the Rebellion," "The Invention of Triage," "The Mills, Fall River, Massachusetts," and "Amelia Earhart, July 2, 1937" in *Lost Coast Review*
"Sunday Afternoon at the Museum of Natural History" in *Broken Bridge Review*
"Her Chinese Robe" and "Eve's Garden" in *White Pelican Review*
"Pumpkin Picking" in *The Alembic*
"Shoebox, Sand, Shells" in *Slipstream*
"Waking the Dead" in *The Emily Dickinson Award Anthology*
"The Dream Factory" in *Awakenings Review*
"Pin Point, Georgia" in *Southern Poetry Review*
"The Frame Shop" in *Birmingham Poetry Review*
"My Father's Heart" in *The South Carolina Review*
"Persephone Speaks" in *ArtWord Quarterly*
"The Boneyard, Wassaw Island" in *Calliope*

Publisher: Leah Maines
Editor: Christen Kincaid
Cover Art: John A. Middleton, Jr.
Author Photo: Patricia L. Farless
Cover Design: Elizabeth Maines McCleavy

Printed in the USA on acid-free paper.
Order online: www.finishinglinepress.com
        also available on amazon.com

Author inquiries and mail orders:
Finishing Line Press
P. O. Box 1626
Georgetown, Kentucky 40324
U. S. A.

Table of Contents

Tin Can Candle 1
The House Comes Apart 3
Home On Your Back 5
Phantom Limbs 7
Eve's Garden 8
Persephone Speaks 9
Pin Point, Georgia 10
Sunday Afternoon at the Museum of Natural History 11
My Father's Heart 13
Pumpkin Picking 14
The Frame Shop 15
Framing the Moon 16
The Dream Factory 17
Interstate 18
Centerville Shoe Store 1965 19
Constructing Border Quilts 20
7,000 pairs of shoes left behind 21
Waking the Dead 22
Radium Girls 23
Emma Livry 1862 24
The Mills, Fall River Massachusetts 25
The Invention of Triage 26
Aiding the Rebellion 27
Amelia Earhart, June 2, 1937 29
Shoebox, Sand, Shells 30
Her Chinese Robe 31
the yellow crane is gone 32
Long March to the Sea 33
The Boneyard, Wassaw Island 34

Tin Can Candle

Composed of hard letters
its little light flames the fourth rib
making shadows on your heart
When the lungs expand

air is cold as a waterfall
open mouth, breathe, blow it out
The candle in its rusty can still burns
making shadows from a self you can't name

How important the flickering flame is
when the desperate light between your ribs
is all you have to fight the shame
of something that shouldn't be shameful

You have kept it smothered, squeaking like a bird caught in a chimney
Confessions do not make winter beauty
from the mundane murmurs of sand, soda, ash
Church glass stretches out, stained in blood and weeping

Waiting just behind your teeth
spill of secrets, spell of dangerous
desires that skate past your tongue
stripping the carefully laid veneer off your body

There is a time for everything
except this singing dissolution:
the self grows larger in the candle's rusty can
and does not fit your middle-class home

Magnifying the conversation you can't take back
smoky words leave your mouth and hang in the silence
until finally they rise and fall
a sheet snapped hard over a marriage bed

Hours later, spent and strangely wounded
you stand next to the retention pond
and watch a heron spear a fat fish
its beak expands rings in the water

Before it swallows, its ancient eyes tell you
there is little mercy in the world
The flame dances in your palm
and you move forward as if walking to the sea

The House Comes Apart

From the outside at street level
it looked as if all my days and months
my lithe body in my little wooden house
imploded all at once.
As if I had not spent years
examining each stone and piece of shiplap
tile, threshold and furring strip.
Each sharp nail, each piece of glass
scrutinized, disarticulated and put back in place
in careful lines, a design that felt civilized
with a structure of ordered domesticity
like cornflakes for breakfast or waffles
with syrup, hot coffee, bedtime stories
laundry, folding socks and late night television
sex twice a week, a large glass of water before bed.
Civilized until it felt no longer tenable.

Looking back the deterioration started
before marriage and children
long performances like dating and senior prom
lipstick, skirts, uncomfortable shoes
sported heels that could take out an eye
if it became necessary or desirable.
Boys I kissed never knowing if the cold
I felt was what I should feel, if desire
was nothing but my imagination.

I ran from every other possibility:
Moruna who left lipstick kisses on paper
poems I would hold to my lips and imagine
the smell of her island skin.
Angie who scared me with her angry hunger
the absence of fear in her heart
thinking *crazy* while I watched her bust up a television
with a hammer until I would do much worse.

The destruction was soul shaking
all the missing pieces rained down
down into a muck of salted tears
and sharp years like debris settled
around my throat until I could no longer breathe.

When I opened the door
the knob fell into my palm
the brass roundness of it
a ball of strength in my hand
I did the bright thing that needed to be done
I left with the metal knob, holding my daughters' small hands
As the streetlights made white moons in the snow
we descended like Pluto into the night

Home on Your Back

Every horizon is an invitation to start over
you remember this line as you make coffee
in the French press you unpacked earlier
You can't remember who told you this
or if at the time it helped

From the back porch, you look east
to the yet unopened sky
partially blocked with shrill green needles
huge pale gray clouds hover overhead
a hint of pale yellow showing through
You will see morning before light sparkles across the marsh
with its smells of sawgrass, earth, decay

not what your roots know
Anxiously your toes curl
origins thin and pale under the balls of your feet
crimped inside your soul, not ready to dig down
to connect the familiar
with the unfamiliar

Behind you, boxes sit unopened
full of kitchen things wrapped in newspapers
furniture pushed into empty spaces
You will trip over chairs for weeks
until muscle memory takes over
and you make what you have carried here
home, another home

The only familiar sound is your breathing
orange brushes of words from other mornings
trapped in warm coffee, you hold
your youngest daughter balanced
on your hip, head buried in your neck and shoulder
her sticky sweet drool mixes with new smells

You try to imagine this is the place you live
your baby child oblivious of the world outside
her immediate view
encased in the husk of half sleep
her scent as known as your own

love me big she mumbles into to your cheek.

A Cooper's hawk flies over head, named for you
by the long sweep of its wings, the white tips of feathers
a predator you have seen before
You take refuge in its shadow
stretch your left arm wide like a bridge
girded between before and now
"This big," you tell your daughter, "this big"

Phantom Limbs

When you have burned your life down
to nothing

it takes a long time, years of reaching out
before the bird whistles

With or without feathers, the sifting
through ashes, burnt bone, table legs

is difficult work: a shoe lace, a blue button, scraps of leaf colored silk
you don't remember wearing

Memories you can't recover, sing and itch like phantom limbs
you feel but cannot see

The eggs you crack for breakfast
held promise once

Eve's Garden

Early sun slips along in slow examination
of an empty branch, the few hard berries
left from November, the empty suet holder.
Morning lightens the promise—
the brave red of robin feathers
the pale lavender crocus fingers—
and pushes aside the last small snows
the last relief of godly rest.

How did the wild do its feasting
in the woods, in the pond
before the hand-feeding of fish and bird?
before the slow, back-breaking digging
the rolling out of rough stone for fences
as wilderness became field, then pasture
then gentle backyards held in place
with rocks low easing?

April voices peel winter sleep from our eyes and hair—
like thick flannel stripped from startled limbs
like the opening of Pandora's box—
flooding the earth with possible desires.
In the nakedness of our garden's makings
long ago sins and volcanic upheavals
live with our recent mapping of earth
and we begin the birthing, the planting, the prayer.

Persephone Speaks

This is what
despair feels like.
From the moist wall of the cave
my voice hollows back
the repetition lichen thin
a timbre just short
of hysteria.
Even the great myths have left
seeping through sandstone
with the river's subterranean passages.
Not for me the ability
to compress a hard ball of clay
into the glory of the sun
to lift the great weight of the sky
on muscled shoulders.
For me lies the responsibility of winter
under dark dormancy
nurturing seed.

Pin Point, Georgia

The historian divides Pin Point into three parts:
Sweet Eden Fields Church, the social hall, the A. S. Varn Cannery.
But the historian's view is architectural, three dimensional,
unlike the language of crab nets,
artifacts that slip in and out of science
wily as a confession before Sunday morning.
It is fishing that shapes time and place on Pin Point
oysters in the fall, crabs in the spring.
The crab nets cannot fill in the difference
between story and history. The distance is unimportant
to memories of marsh, river, inlet, bateaux, cracked shells
these things bound in the soul like yeast.
Collecting others' stories, like freeing oysters,
opens muscled hearts, finds their secret tongues.
John Henry Haines has been a waterman
his whole life. At eighty, he makes his own nets
tying the ends taunt to the porch railing
and knitting a round, sonorous shape
strings seductive as a wedding skirt.
The crabs have no memory and cannot escape the nets' pull.
Nets fall around the crab pink bodies
moist as their own skin,
but holes are knitted large enough
for souls and stars to slip through.
Smelling cold and sharp as aluminum pans
stars light the beetle shell sky covering the marsh.
John Henry sees a map of the waterways for the first time
and cannot imagine the world the size of a piece of paper
laid out all at once. Her water knowledge depends solely on memory
the gestures of marsh grass, riptides, the slow left turn of inlet
and tide, the holy bottle green light of early spring
that promises crabs and kin.

Sunday Afternoon at the Museum of Natural History

> *There are no words that can tell the hidden spirit of the wilderness that can reveal its mystery, its melancholy, its charm.*
> —Theodore Roosevelt (1858-1919)

The Sunday afternoon walk around Central Park
finds Jane and me at the museum studying Teddy Roosevelt
an early pioneer of the conservation movement.
The rotunda holds echoes of exploration and animal ghosts
memories of a million eras of seas and rocks—
Precambrian Paleozoic Mesozoic
and what slithered from the oceans in shorter periods—
Silurian Devonian Carboniferous the age of coniferous plants
the time from Jurassic to Paleocene when mammals evolved.

In the Akeley Hall of African Mammals
we learn species *a category of biological classification that follows*
genus *a class logically divided into several subordinate species*

Here all life is hierarchical.

Victorian hunters—Sir Walter Reynolds, the Earl of Sudbury, Sir Thomas Hamilton—
have made gifts now housed in dioramas
windows on habitats, brown deserts and savannahs
twists of leaf—olive emerald olive—a bit of yellow
feather like flashes of sun and the underbelly of turtles
showcase Akeley's artisan skill with wire, clay, and colored glass eyes.
    genus *Bovidae*
    species *antelope*
bodies lighter and racier than oxen
with horns that sprout upward and back
Tapis horns grow short and straight, church steeples for the frightened.

We learn to tell antelope apart by horn shapes—
Gemsbock, hoofs in gritty sand, sport pointed horns curved like banisters.
The horns of Sable antelopes spread wide and sharp like scimitars.
Hartebeest horns spiral, extruded ribbon candy
while Impala horns look like shells turned inside out.
In the grasslands graze the Greater Kudu wearing barley twists as hats.

All the same species look out at us

with dull, marble eyes, that watch grazing land shrink
smaller and smaller to the size of glass houses.
Inside antelope forever stretch
their parched throats
yearning for the scent of water.

My Father's Heart

This plot anticipates more than an oldest daughter can shoulder.
In the terrible order of siblings, the relief of details,
the things I must take care of occupy my mind and hands refusing tears.

My role has been virtually cast for decades,
but there is comfort in the familiar precision of family:
the meals cooked, the socks washed, the arrangements made.

My relation with my father's heart
allows no arguments. The EKG marks the beats, the pauses.
No questions, no quarrels mar the inked peaks,

this scribbling of foreign monks,
how doctors read hearts because it's all they know.
Their fingers trace the hills and valleys, circle his life.

The cardiologist holds a map in his hands—
my father's heart colonized by medicine. Yet, inside his chest
the ways of our family inhabit whole regions.

In the spent light of the afternoon, black ink shadows
the paper folds in a soft whoosh of fall leaves,
pastel tones call the different names of his children.

Their white faces orbit his bed, speechless moons
for there are no moments in our language
to describe the less than holy versions of who we are.

Pumpkin Picking

Up the gravel drive
the promised autumn hill
is thickly sprinkled joy
of sun eggs, broken stars
and fire seeds.
My daughters hunt for possibilities:
one searches with nurse hands
her fingertips feel for bumps
rough spots, the loose twists
of umbilical stems.
The other springs over orange mounds
finds a pumpkin larger than herself
forty pounds at least, I think.
I tell her only as big as you can pick up.
She begins to roll that one to the car
its sides soon spotted with mud and gravel.
Her braid twitches down her back
blue black of witch's night.

My older daughter
brings me a smaller pumpkin
more green than orange
a soft brown spot near its base.
We could put the mouth there.
She tells me, no one else will want her
she'll die here.
I think of the pumpkin broken in the field
her meat picked by feeding birds
her flat seeds, hundreds of potential children
fallen, then flying to life inside the soil.
There are worse fates.
I nod assent, she smiles.
We run down the drive to catch her sister.

The Frame Shop

Painstakingly peeling off the yellowed tape
she'd used to hold the photo in place
he tells her, "This tape is not archival."
The photo is, she supposes. Wildwood, New Jersey
in 1927, more softened in color, more color, more solemn in face
then she remembered their summers. The striped bathing clothes
she and her brother wear cover most of their white limbs.
This is what it means to grow old, she muses, one notices
changes in fashions over decades rather than from week to week.
He splays a peacock fan of matting on the counter in front of her.
She is almost obsessed with the desire to choose
the perfect color matting:
a shadow of brown marsh grass in winter
and the thin green layer of old brass.
Patina, she remembers, verdigris.
She knows all the words for aging.
The corners of the photos are curved, cracking
he cuts the mat to cover the edges. She watches
the movement of his razor knife, the sharp bone in his right wrist.
The thin sound of knife cleaving mat cuts the air
with the sureness of Parsons' ammonia.
Being human is such a complicated task, she thinks.
The eyes of the children in the photograph
remind her that it is not enough to be born.
The waves in the background are faded beyond recognition
sea finally blending into sky.

Framing the Moon

It has been years, but I feel like I should explain
about getting lost the evening
we drove around that housing development searching
for something familiar in our new lives.
Every home looked the same, timed to darken before dusk.
The neighborhood built so recently, there were no street signs
and few comforting house numbers.
We were dependent upon directions with no phone number
scribbled on school paper by your new friend.
You were to spend the night at her house
though we had spent so little time at our own.
I yelled at you about not getting better directions
as the lawn sprinklers came on in unison
sounding like silk singing over the grass.
My anger at your navigation wasn't fair
for I was more lost than I could tell you,
couldn't tell you that even parents
feel alone and afraid sometimes,
and I had become more vulnerable
to little things like sprinklers
and stars that were not my own.
The moon came up from behind your friend's house
catching us like doe's eyes
in the unexpectedness of reflected light.
You opened the car door
and in that moment before your leaving
I searched for the right combination
of light, subject, background, framing,
words to hold the moon's movement still,
to enfold us in the speed of a camera's shutter.

The Dream Factory

We spent last week searching
your mind for clues,
the correctable defects.
You forget your name sometimes,
where you are, losing the here,
loosening focus, while limbs jazz
your fingers and convulsions dance
on mornings when you waken
slower than insect whine or bird song.

The MRI scan photo-slices your brain like deli meat
in layers of optic nerve, cerebrum, cerebellum, sinus walls,
coils of mind flesh flat on the monitor screen. It's a kind of torture, slicing
your brain open like this, looking for secrets. You fight, hanging
onto your hidden folds, leaving round heel bruises on my chest
and arms, scratching my neck through the cotton fog of anesthesia.
This is only fair—after all, I brought you here.

It's the misplaced lines, the narrow ghosts and near misses
from EEG tracings that look most like patterns of dreaming.
These are your dreams seen from the outside.
The lines are all sharply angled, South-
western topography, the beige starkness of sand-covered
knees and elbows, hard nipples without the round softness
of breast or thigh, no purple-bellied clouds, no pale shadows
smother the peaks for coherent contrast.
There is no sun; we cannot see that your patterns
of dreaming come in the day as well as the night.
I color inside the lines.
The spiked patterns curved like wishes you seek to fulfill
making the real into the imaginary,
the imaginary into the real.

Later at home I watch robins, puppet heads
pulling insects from the lawn. They hide bird dreams behind eyes
determined as buttons, caches for the inside of clouds.

Interstate

Black lines on yellowed paper
stand in place of magic

I read to my grandmother
the directions to the next town

She flicks her cigarette out the window
turns on the car radio, calls me "butter bean"

Nothing but static and farm reports
we've been looking for music for hours

the Stones "She's a Rainbow" or
Janis Joplin, her blues worse than ours

My sister sleeps, slumped in the back seat
her face flushed and hair stuck to one cheek

The sky to the west begins to cloud and ash
the moon appears, a soft dusty thumbprint

Later when we have crossed into another state
it will grow to a perfect silver disk

Centerville Shoe Store, 1965

While the other girls wore
saddle shoes, the black then white winking
or shiny penny loafers
bright copper seducing the hallway
heels tap dancing on the worn green tiles

Always take care of your feet, my father warned
Under his tutelage that meant
brown oxfords, Buster Brown and his bulldog, Tige
These were boys' shoes as far as I knew
no matter what the sales lady said

I pouted, I cried, I begged
I refused to buy shoes
way past the age when a yellow lollipop
Poll Parrot clicker or cardboard hat
would mollify my fashion sense

Always take care of your feet, I heard his voice
and laughed when I bought my own shoes—
Spike heeled leather boots, blue and white pumps
red skyscraper platforms, gold sparkly sandals—
all designed to keep a woman's feet off balance

My father flew a B-29 Superfortress in Korea
By 25 in leather flight jacket and googles
he knew what monsters could coil and spit in the cloudless sky
what mammoths roiled beneath to buckle
the smoothest sidewalk

Constructing Border Quilts

> *"The Migrant Quilt Project believes in art and activism. The quilt-makers sew quilts out of migrants discarded clothes found in the desert and embroider them with the names of migrants who died while attempting the journey."*
> —Angela Martinez, 2018

looking for justice with thread, pins, needle
and scissors, cutting shirts and dungarees abandoned
out of necessity for the weight of the journey
sharp mountains, miles of windy desert
the owners needing to carry water and food
more than excess clothing and empty *bordados*

the quilt pieced still looks like clothing
so one can read these quilts as covering
the brown limbs of individuals walking
so one can protest the erasure of people who wore them
lament their lives and thirsty feet funneled to America

who walked from poverty
who walked away from injustice
who walked from certain death
to possible death

their full names embroidered
or *desconocido* on material
torn and stained with blood

a little girl's pink dress carefully mended
stitched next to her mother's ripped blouse

a woman leaving her shoes behind and running

7,000 pairs of shoes left behind

and laid to rest in a fan shape
on the brittle March grass
in the background, the front of the capitol building
glows clean white, the dome golden in the sun
a faux benediction to the dead
the frame resonates with sympathy
—there's nothing more painful than a lost person's shoes
stopped in step, many or few doesn't matter
they won't be repeated
the ghost rhythm resonates in the empty shoes
canvas or leather holds the foot's shape
heel, sole, toes, the arch's curve specific to the foot

you are supposed to notice the overwhelming number
of those killed by gun violence
but your eyes rest on the little pink sneakers
white elephants painted on the toes
you can't look away
from the child's little feet
the fingers that made the bunny ear
and tied the bow

Waking the Dead

Why don't you write a poem about kudzu?
She laughs asking me this
on the drive between Macon and Atlanta
her voice echoing in the car's closed consciousness.
Where the kudzu grows both north and south bound
the highway streams between green, ghost town silences.

Do travelers see kudzu or only the shadows it leaves behind?
Fat leaves cover the fences, posts and shacks lining the highway.
Tough vines smother the shapes of thick armed
Southern pines, a halleluiah of hoary gods
arching limbs fearless as dragon bones and ancestors
prickly needles distinct as spirits and layers of memory.

Instead I tell her about other car trips
between New Haven and Providence
every Thanksgiving eve of my childhood
half listening to the cadence of my parents' rosary
we drove past factories, prisons and schools
cloaked in the same dull red brick.

Outside of New London just before dusk
we'd reach *All Souls Cemetery* where my brothers and I held
our breath, lifted our feet high into our bellies
until the car passed the last iron curled gate. We'd explode
in air and the drum of Keds hitting the car floor.
My mother would turn her head. *You'll wake the dead,* she'd say.

I tell her about my older brother's sucked in cheeks
and how he'd let his breath out in one long whistle.
Behind my parents' call and response *almighty maker of heaven and earth*
his face faded behind his freckles, the whistle already gone
and holy before it ended, nostalgic as a train calling
lost in the distant gray sky.

Radium Girls

Licking the paint brush to a fine tip
she dipped it in the greenish glow
of radio luminescent paint
and carefully outlined the numbers
on the gentleman's watch
so he could tell time in the dark
while waving for a cab, rushing home to his wife
white scarf wrapped around the collar
of his cashmere wool coat
maybe she knitted it
each stitch with "he loves me"

She smiled to herself
and dipped the brush again
her favorite jobs were instrument panels
she imagined the pilots flying
through the night on missions of mercy
their faces lit by her soft brushstrokes
flying food to Senegal, polio vaccines to Brazil
she liked to think of heroes
before she had to become one

before the radium she had ingested
infected her jaw, making her gums bleed, her teeth loosen
The doctors called it *radium-induced osteonecrosis*
some of the girls from the plant died
the investigators showed how the workroom glowed
when the lights were turned off
the desks, chairs, shelves all glowed
but worse, far worse bodies glowed
hands, faces, arms, legs, necks, even her hair
and she had just washed it that morning

The next day she brought in her clothes
all of it, everything she owned in carried the ghoulish light
even after laundering her underwear
it glowed and they had never said
radium is dangerous
it could make you sick

Emma Livry, 1862

Eyes pulled tight behind spectacles
a young newspaper artist strains to see
across the stage of the Paris Opéra House
seeking a story, a movement he tries but cannot
capture with his tight charcoal lines on drawing paper
In the wings where she waits
the air is thinner, the light plaintive

her body stripped of everything, distilled
to a romantic presence, flesh consumed by art

Her lightness, her light is everything
and in everything like a flicker, like a sun

A plain girl with a doll's body
when still—skinny limbs, too large elbows
collarbones jutting from her neck
—until she dances in *Le Papillon*
the butterfly princess attracted to light

Except butterflies are not attracted to light

This night silken tutu and tight corset outline
her graceful moves, she steps out of her robe
it falls to the back stage floor like a whisper
and she floats over the floor too close to the gas lightening
a final fluff of her skirt, costume instantly aflame
and the harsh tang of fear, like the skin of a walnut
lined her tongue, *en pointe* as fire burned her wings

and the artist draws her out there in ashes
where the dead wave in memory of light

The Mills, Fall River, Massachusetts

> *But he did not answer her a word. And his disciples came and begged him, saying, "Send her away, for she is crying after us."*
> *—Matthew 15: 24*

There is a certain industry in madness
the din of two hundred shuttle cocks
slamming wooden bobbins back and forth
forth and back. Madness weaves thick
red threads that nest her yellow throat
making it hard to breathe
harder still to speak up.
The rumble of civilization spins
round and round and there's never enough to eat.

Her mother prays for the faith to understand entropy
the rush of wind through a nun's stuffy room.
What portion of the world's weight must she carry?
Her daughter runs across the wooden floor, heaving
spools of thread larger than her thin bruised arms.
She ducks under her mother's quick feet, under the metal treadles
of the patient sewing machine marching its way across linen.
Even the dogs under the table can lick the children's crumbs.

Faith is not the temperate angel breath that lifts
the folded wings of one thousand paper cranes.
Faith is the hours, the nights and days of bending
folding sharp creases, creases cut with scissors
brown, blue, green triangles, tiny pains like split skin
one quick pull, a balance of beak and tail
right wing and left wing, tacking cotton bodice to sleeve.
She carries one white crane in her palm
the rest follow behind in a steady stream.

Canaan dust settles on her mother's seamed face
the long road kicked up by the tiny mercies of her feet.
She pleads, "my daughter is severely possessed."
Blinded by bird wings and the Israelites' needs, Jesus looks away.

Her mother screams a prayer to the foreman's God
echoing the ache from one thousand asylums—
"I will have justice for my daughter."
The divine, expanded in her human pain, gathers in the birds
the flash of wings blows the dust from her daughter's eyes.

The Invention of Triage

> "The most melancholy spectacle that one can imagine meets the eye here—
> Houses dismantled and torn to pieces, gardens ruined and trampled down,
> fences torn away, orchards destroyed, and indeed all marks of civilization and
> culture lost. Such is one of the many curses & horrors of war."
> —Major Richard Maury, 24th Virginia, March 1862, Fairfax Station

Edges of dogwood leaves turn tinged brown and yellow.
September morning holds a sky still azure from summer.
Breezes left from last night's storm turn the grass like flirting eyelashes
brown birds, singing their piercing forest opera stopped by the sudden
round sound of cart wheels, tired hooves, shuffling broken boots
leather scrapping earth and stone.

We knew more soldiers would come in torn, bloody blue and gold
on foot, on horseback, by the wagon load, their groans
storm our small rail station, like the sounds of animals
sent to slaughter. Immersed in the coppery smells of blood
the stink of vomit, of urine, we shiver in the growing heat of day.
We learn to sort men like spoiled apples.

Following Clara's lead, those we could save went on the first trains.
Those who could walk helped carry the wounded, sprawled their bent
bloody bodies on splintered planks torn from houses and fences
in Chantilly and Ox Hill and Blackburn's Ford, where cannon balls
tore through the bones of homes, the bones of men leaving jagged wounds
white splinters, red streams, blue uniforms.

Eight thousand different wounds, though their eyes suffered all the same.
The ones who could grab our dusky skirts, hems dirty with mud
(cotton petticoats long since ripped into bandages and tourniquets)
those soldier boys rewarded with jewels of jam, scoops of blue and red
from harvest, (our fingers like silver spoons) and sips of water, sherry
fruit wines from women's afternoons.

Hours ago, one would barely know we were at war with ourselves.
Out of bandages, we tear our knickers, yellowed shifts, and cover limbs
we promise will be there tomorrow and next week—an arm, a leg, a lone foot,
the boy not knowing the other is already gone. Under the makeshift wrappings,
invisible infections break down their skin like bird shot. We pray and bandage
boys' bodies and feel young chests for quickening hearts.

Aiding the Rebellion

Sybil Ludington, April 26, 1777

April in New York is planting season:
the Colonel's regiment disbanded to plow an earth
moist with snow melt, drifting promise of hay and feed corn.
Sybil finished her kitchen chores, tightly tucked her smaller siblings
under the blue and yellow quilt her mother thought looked like spring.
With a lullaby, her whispery alto made them sleepy:

> *Darkness falls, sand man calls, go to sleep my little baby.*
> *When you wake, you shall have all the pretty little horses.*

She thought she could smell the smoke and imagined
orange, yellow and red flames from the British attack
on Danbury's stores. The war raged only seventeen miles
from the Ludington farm. She heard her father's heavy
voice vibrate through the crossbeams, the river stone chimney
voices swift as water, the fire of men with ideals.

> *Blacks and bays, dapples and greys, go to sleep little baby*

Children, chickens, sweet corn could not hold
the passion inside as she flew down the stairs
and offered to summon her father's soldiers.

Newly sixteen, barely old enough to be the revolution's oracle
her father mapped the route for his Cassandra, a route she knew
with her eyes closed, along with a few forest shortcuts discovered
with Luke, but she wisely kept those afternoons to herself.
Sybil's white thighs clung to a saddle
slick with animal sweat and her own trembling thoughts.

She left Fredericksburg just after dark
steered Star south and west
and rode fast on narrow, unmarked roads
until dew formed, bending the grass towards morning.
She thought of Luke and his warm fingers on her cheek
without the moon, the blushing thoughts a warmer cloak.

Her warning a ferocious banging on militia doors
with the same stick she used to spur Star harder

past nests of small twigs, pale green with spring's restlessness
branches snap and grab, she answers the woods unwelcoming howls
fighting off deserters and highway men with her father's musket.
Cramped and chilled after ten hours of hard riding
of muddy woods and cold drizzle
shivering down her neck, soaking her skin.

Homesteads, hamlets, farms, fences and barns
blurred together in her exhausted eyes. Forty miles
through Carmel to Mahopac, onto Kent Cliffs and Farmers Mills
then finally home where 400 armed men stood outside her door
ready to march General Tyron back to the Sound.
For a brief moment Sybil felt more alive than ever before
breathing the scent of freedom, while warm biscuits
fresh eggs, earth and a scratchy flannel sleeve
filled her senses as Luke gently lifted her from Star's back.

Amelia Earhart, July 2, 1937

> "'It's the classic desert island,' Gillespie said. 'It's beautiful to look at...
> and it hurts all the time.'"

She smiles for the camera with lips sealed
chin turned and placed over her left shoulder
disheveled hair finger brushed from her forehead
poised uncomfortably on earth. It is early March 1937, Los Angeles
inside the cockpit of her Lockheed Electra. She is sitting to the right
of the altimeter, fuel gauge, clock roundly fill the left of the photograph
and most of the center, technology claims space from her eyes.

Richard Gillespie holds this photograph next to his own face.
It is early March 1992, and he has found her shoe, brown, size nine
a pill bottle, and part of the plane's metal fuselage on Nikumaroro Island.
What he has unearthed after his four-year search for her death is the remnant
of one shoe, a black heel of Cat's Paw rubber.

Failing to "find her destination," Earhart and her navigator, Fred Noonan
landed on an atoll, its shores littered with sharp shell fragments
that sliced open shoes and feet. For three days, Gillespie theorizes,
they sent distress signals until a storm "swept" the plane
"over the edge of the reef into deep water." Three days hearing her watch
prick time, the tiny hands like needles of coral, three days of little water
in 120-degree temperatures, watching the plane breakup in the sea.

Shoebox, Sand, Shells

I have held this box of shells
through five or six states
and more years than I want to name.
The thin cardboard has crumbled
and broken from love's waiting.
With one finger I stir and sift
for an ivory shell, shaped round with desire.
"It looks like a breast," you said.
I can still hear your laugh
chin cupped in my open palms
as another reminded you of a vulva
and reminded me of the way you tasted
of sweetness and sea salt
my tongue wrapped inside you—
even then I hoarded memories.
The gritty Nantucket sand stuck to your thighs
with coconut oil rubbed my cheeks pink.
Your body a mosaic of oceans and wind
and the small scented cries of hungry gulls.

Her Chinese Robe

There are pieces of your life with her in three countries:
jewelry, books, single socks, snapped guitar strings
tracing a forensics of paper strands, skin slips, snares of hair
old photos that whisper and sigh like yellowed leaves.
On the cover photo of her new CD you find
your red Converse hi-tops laced to her feet.
You'd forgotten the sneakers, holly berry red
favored for one season, then lost the winter you let her go.
From the balcony you watched her walk away
feet breaking holy rivers through the wet snow
and her city voice, fragile as glass, breathing the brittle air.
Since the thaw, you've lived alone
and wondered with each sighing pipe, each trickling faucet
why she took your pipe wrench and your favorite screwdriver.

You left Montreal in late summer carrying her white Chinese robe
and each winter wear her silk chrysanthemum dreams to bed
memories embroidered in autumn's imitation gold.
In the awful moments before sleep, the calluses on your fingers
read the raised petals like fine Braille mourning notes.
You rest in a breakable world, in the elusiveness of sound.
After breakfast, your hands lost to warm water and dish soap
you clean coffee grounds and sponge toast crumbs
from the single cup, the single plate, the single spoon.
Overwhelmed by longing and the immediacy of dreams
your hands stroke her body slippery and moist
a sea star opens to your fingers and mouth
and your soul folds around her blue shadowed scent
curved like a comma, sleep's sentence unfinished.

the yellow crane is gone

in the blue of nightfall
his handwriting opens slowly
intimate as skin

and the rain
when it comes
is not what he expected

on this hill where he is banished
he watches the sky swallow the crane
bends to write "what if there is no other place?"

The Long March to the Mountain

In three poems by Mao
the mountains are at the beginning
of the sky and river.

The mountains keep the sky from collapsing
when the sea and river boil over.
He crosses mountains on his war pony.

The snow, the sky, the warm breath of horses
wreaths the peaks as he sits. There is no peace
when watching other men on horseback in fierce battle.

Dali drew these horses with red bridles
and wavy manes, teeth set to bite
their rumps and thighs, circles on circles.

Dali's horses are wild, riderless, alone
as if there had been no war, no boiling river
no mountains in his drawing for Mao.

The Boneyard, Wassaw Island

We name the place with our marrow
wooden bones revised by sun bleach and fast air.
Spaces that hold sacred another's pain, hold the walking through
arthritic hip twists and elbow branches that ghost my living flesh.

We stand between histories: the waves keep
and sound decisions already made
choices still to make.

We mark raccoon prints, delicate tracings
point to language offshore
chart the knowing when to leave
what to leave behind.

Martha Catherine Brenckle is a Professor at the University of Central Florida where she teaches First-year Writing and Rhetorical Theory. She writes poetry and fiction and has published most recently in *The Sea Letter, Clockhouse Review, Broken Bridge Review, Burningword Literary Magazine,* and *Bryant Literary Review* among others. In 2000, she won the Central Florida United Arts Award for Poetry. Martha is a former performance poet and has performed her monologues on lesbian life in Orlando, Tampa, Atlanta, New Haven, New Orleans, Chicago, San Antonio, and Baltimore. Her first novel, *Street Angel* (2006), was nominated for a Lambda Award and a Triangle Award and was a Finalist for *Fence Magazine*'s 2007 Best GLBT Novel Award. She lives in Winter Park, FL with her wife Patty and their gray tabby cats.

www.ingramcontent.com/pod-product-compliance
Lightning Source LLC
LaVergne TN
LVHW041601070426
835507LV00011B/1228